Home Run King

by Steven Otfinoski

MODERN CURRICULUM PRESS

Pearson Learning Group

It was a brisk evening in early September, 1998, in St. Louis's Busch Stadium. The stadium was filled to capacity. The St. Louis Cardinals were playing the Chicago Cubs.

But the most important thing on the minds of most fans that night was not who would win the game. All eyes were on Mark McGwire, the large, red-headed first baseman for the Cardinals.

That night the fans were waiting to witness baseball history. Over the hot Labor Day weekend McGwire had become the third major league player to hit sixty home runs in one season.

The other two players were Babe Ruth and Roger
Maris. In 1961, Maris had broken Ruth's record with
sixty-one home runs. On Labor Day, McGwire hit his
sixty-first home run to tie Maris's record. It was a birthday
present to his father, John McGwire, who turned sixty-one
that same day.

Now all of America was rooting for McGwire to break
Maris's thirty-seven year record and become the Home Run
King. His first time at bat, McGwire grounded out to
shortstop. In the fourth inning, he was up at bat again. The
Cardinals had two men out and no one on base.

McGwire walked to the plate and got into position. The whole stadium was quiet. The tension in the air was unbelievable. The pitcher wound up and threw the ball. The ball sped eighty-eight miles per hour toward the plate. McGwire swung his bat. Crack! Ball and bat connected.

The ball sailed toward left field, clearing the stadium wall by just five feet. Then it hit a sign and dropped from sight. This was the record-breaking homer everyone had been waiting for. It would also be the shortest home run of McGwire's incredible season, traveling a distance of only 341 feet.

The fans went wild. Even the umpire was excited. The cheers were deafening as McGwire slowly rounded the bases in the blinding light of hundreds of flashing cameras.

When he finally reached home plate, the entire Cardinals team was there to greet him. Mark's ten-year-old son, Matthew, was there too.

A player for the Cubs came running from the field toward McGwire. It was Sammy Sosa. For weeks, McGwire and Sosa had been neck-and-neck in the home-run race. The competition had been a friendly one, and the two men shared a deep respect for one another. Now they hugged warmly. No one could have been happier for McGwire than his number-one rival, Sammy Sosa.

McGwire also wanted to share this moment with another group of people. Sitting nearby were Roger Maris's six grown children. They had come to see McGwire break their father's record. He went over and hugged each one of them.

Mark McGwire had been born on October 1, 1963, two years to the day after Roger Maris hit his sixty-first home run. Throughout the 1998 season, McGwire had spoken of Maris with great respect.

Roger Maris had never gotten the respect that Mark McGwire was now receiving. At the time, many people were upset with him for breaking Babe Ruth's record. Now McGwire's triumph was reviving interest in Maris's memory and earning him respect too.

    While McGwire was receiving the cheers of the crowd, something else was going on in the stadium. A groundskeeper had found the ball he hit. He rushed it to the Cardinals' office.

    A short time later, officials came to the office with a special lamp. When the lamp was turned on the baseball, the ink glowed. It was McGwire's home run ball!

Officials wanted to make sure they could identify McGwire's home run balls. Every ball pitched to McGwire after his fifty-ninth home run had been covered with a special ink. When placed under a special infrared light, the ink would glow. This would prove that each ball was the one that McGwire had used to hit a home run.

McGwire gave the baseball to the Baseball Hall of Fame, along with the bat he used and the uniform he wore.

Over the few remaining weeks of the baseball season, he hit eight more home runs. He hit the last two in the last game of the season. This brought the total to seventy. During that time, Sammy Sosa also broke Maris's record with a season total of sixty-six home runs.

"It's a huge number. It's unheard of," McGwire said after hitting number seventy. "I'm in awe of myself right now."

Anyone who knows Mark McGwire knows he wasn't bragging. Despite his great achievements, he is not haughty or temperamental. He is a team player with a good attitude. He even gets along with the umpire—usually.

He cares about children too. He is a model father to his own son, Matthew, and helped him become a bat boy for the Cardinals, so the two could be together more.

Mark cares about other children as well. He gives autographs and time to young fans whenever he can. He also has started his own foundation for abused children.

These good qualities and his athletic skills have made Mark McGwire a hero to many Americans. He has shown us that a great athlete doesn't have to be haughty and arrogant.

Baseball wasn't always Mark's favorite sport. As a youngster growing up in Claremont, California, he liked golf and soccer. That changed in high school.

"Mark wasn't afraid to work," says his high school baseball coach. "He worked hard, and that set him apart."

Baseball was important to Mark, but his parents made sure that it didn't run his life. When he went to the University of Southern California, his baseball coach recognized that fact. "He was very unselfish, very disciplined, and was a great teammate, and that comes from having wonderful parents," his coach said. "You learn that from your parents."

In 1984, McGwire was drafted by the Oakland Athletics. When he left the team in 1997, he had set a team record of 363 home runs. That same year, he was traded to the St. Louis Cardinals.

Mark McGwire's achievement was a victory for himself and for the sport of baseball. After the players' strike of 1994–1995, many people said baseball would never again be America's favorite pastime. Mark McGwire, the Home Run King, proved them wrong. People's interest in baseball was renewed by this great American slugger. The excitement and grandeur of the sport returned.

Mark hit his last two homers of the season against the Montreal Expos. After the game, Expos manager Felipe Alan told reporters, "I'm glad the season is over. The way he was swinging, he was on his way to eighty."

Well, there's always next season!